NEW EDITION

Wide Range Readers

BLUE BOOK 1

Fred J. Schonell
Phyllis Flowerdew

Oliver & Boyd

Illustrate by Andrew Brownfoot, Pamela Goodchild, Tony Herbert, Nicholas Hewetson, Carol Holmes, Caroline Sharpe, Gwen Tourret and Pat Tourret.

Oliver & Boyd
Longman House
Burnt Mill
Harlow
Essex CM20 2JE

An Imprint of Longman Group UK Ltd

First published 1948
Second edition 1965
Third edition 1976
Fourth edition 1985
Sixth impression 1991

© Phyllis Flowerdew and the Executors of
the late Sir Fred J. Schonell 1965, 1985
(Except 'Manu and the Fish', 'Nothing Ever
Happens!' and 'How Maui Caught the Great
Sun' © Moira Miller 1985)

All rights reserved; no part of this
publication may be reproduced, stored in
a retrieval system, or transmitted in any
form or by any means, electronic, mechanical,
photocopying, recording, or otherwise, without
either the prior written permission of the
Publishers or a licence permitting restricted
copying in the United Kingdom issued by the
Copyright Licensing Agency Ltd, 33-34 Alfred
Place, London, WC1E 7DP.

Set in 14/20pt 'Monophoto' Plantin

Produced by Longman Group (FE) Ltd
Printed in Hong Kong

ISBN 0-05-003743-9

Preface

The Wide Range Readers are planned to provide graded reading practice for junior school children. Because children of 7–11 have a wide range of reading needs and attainments, there are three parallel series – Blue, Green and Red books – to provide plenty of material to suit the interests and reading ages of every child.

Books 1–4 are graded by half yearly reading ages, for use by appropriate groups within a class. Book 1 should provide an easy read for children with a reading age of about $7-7\frac{1}{2}$. Children with reading ages below 7 are recommended to use the Wide Range Starters.

The controlled vocabulary of the series makes the books suitable for the following reading ages:

$6\frac{1}{2}-7$	**Starter Books**	– Blue, Green and Red
$7-7\frac{1}{2}$	**Book 1**	– Blue, Green and Red
$7\frac{1}{2}-8$	**Book 2**	– Blue, Green and Red
$8-8\frac{1}{2}$	**Book 3**	– Blue, Green and Red
$8\frac{1}{2}-9$	**Book 4**	– Blue, Green and Red
9+	**Book 5**	– Blue, Green and Red
10+	**Book 6**	– Blue, Green and Red
11+	**Book 7**	– Red only
12+	**Book 8**	– Red only

Where to Find the Stories

page

- 5 Strawberry Jam
- 15 Manu and the Fish
- 24 Little Sand Horse
- 40 The Coal Lorry
- 48 The Tortoise Who Talked too Much
- 56 Nothing Ever Happens!
- 68 Martin and the Bear
- 82 The Fisherman and His Wife
- 95 How Maui Caught the Great Sun
- 104 Lucky Hans
- 109 Pussy Willows
- 113 Teddy the Koala
- 126 Sun and Wind

Strawberry Jam

There was once an old woman
who made some strawberry jam.
She stirred it, and she stirred it,
and when it was cooked
she poured it out into some
clean, shining jam jars.

There were ten shining jam jars,
and the strawberry jam dropped
from the saucepan,
plop, plop, plopetty plop,
until the first jar was filled.

Then the jam dropped,
plop, plop, plopetty plop,
until the second jar was filled.
Then the jam dropped,
plop, plop, plopetty plop,
until all the ten jars were filled
right up to the tip top
with red, sticky strawberry jam.

Just enough was left in the saucepan
for the old woman to put on some bread
for her little grandson's supper.
She tied a clean piece of paper
over the top of each jar.
She put them on a shelf in the kitchen
and left them all in a row to cool.

At nine o'clock the old woman
went off to bed.

At half-past nine a tin fell
against the first jam jar
and knocked it on to the second jar.
The second jar fell against the third.
The third fell against the fourth,

and so on, all along the row of jars
until the last jam jar fell on its side,
and there it stayed all night.

Soon the red, sticky strawberry jam
began to come through
the clean paper top. It began
to drip down on to the kitchen floor,
drip, drip, drip, drip!

At ten o'clock, when all was still,
there was a scratching sound
in the corner of the kitchen.
A wee white mouse with pink eyes
and a long pink tail
peeped out of his hole.
He ran across the kitchen floor,
looking for crumbs or bits of bread
that might have been left about.

He had nine baby mice in his nest
at home. He had left them fast asleep.
They were funny little pink things,
with round noses, and white fur
just beginning to grow.

When the sunlight fell on their backs,
they shone like silver.

The wee white father mouse
came near to the place in the kitchen
where the jam was dripping,
drip, drip, drip on to the kitchen floor.
Just as he passed by this place,
a drop of red, sticky strawberry jam
fell splash on the tip of his pink nose.

He licked his nose.
How nice it tasted! He licked it again.
How sweet it was! Oh, how sweet it was!
The wee white mouse thought to himself,
 "I must come back here,
and find more of that nice sticky stuff
when I'm not so busy. I've never
tasted anything so sweet."
He ran away over the kitchen floor.

The red, sticky strawberry jam
dripped to the floor, drip, drip, drip!

Soon there was another
scratching sound in the kitchen,
and a second wee white mouse,
with pink eyes and long whiskers,
crept across the floor. He was
looking for crumbs and bits of bread.
He came near to the place
where the jam was dripping,
drip, drip, drip on to the kitchen floor.
Just as he was passing by, a drop fell
splash on the top of his head.

It didn't stop there, but slipped down
over the sides of his face,
on to his long whiskers.

He licked his whiskers.
How nice they tasted!
He licked them again.
How sweet they were!
The wee white mouse thought to himself,

"I must come back here later
and find more of that nice sweet stuff
when I'm not so busy," and he ran away
over the kitchen floor.

The red, sticky strawberry jam
dripped to the floor, drip, drip, drip!

Soon there was another
scratching sound in the kitchen,
and once more a wee white mouse
with pink eyes and a long pink tail
ran over the kitchen floor.
She came near to the place
where the jam was dripping,
drip, drip, drip on to the floor.

Just as she was passing, a drop fell
splash right on the tip
of her long pink tail.

She twirled her tail round,
and licked it.   How nice it tasted!
She licked it again.   How sweet it was!
The wee white mouse thought to herself,

"I must come back here later
and find more of that nice sweet stuff
when I'm not so busy," and she ran away
over the kitchen floor.

The red, sticky strawberry jam
dripped to the floor, drip, drip, drip.

Now there was a party among the mice
that night at ten o'clock,
in the largest mouse hole, under the floor.
The three wee white mice
who had tasted the red, sticky strawberry
jam, began to tell each other about it.

"A drop of red, sticky stuff
fell on my nose," said the first mouse,
"and it tasted so sweet!"

"A drop of red, sweet stuff
fell on my head and whiskers,"
said the mouse with the long whiskers,
"and it tasted so nice!"

"A drop of red, sweet stuff
fell on the tip of my tail,"
said the mouse with the long tail,
"and it tasted wonderful!"

"Let's look for some more,"
said all the other mice.
"We'll all go to the kitchen together
when the clock strikes twelve."

It was quite a long time
till twelve o'clock, so the mice
had a game of Blind Man's Buff.

Now there was one little mouse,
a greedy little mouse, who just couldn't
wait till twelve o'clock.
She wasn't playing Blind Man's Buff.
So, when no one was looking, she slipped
out of the hole under the floor,
and ran into the kitchen.

The red, sticky strawberry jam
was still dripping, drip, drip, drip

on to the nice, clean kitchen floor.

Just as the little mouse came near,
all the jam that was left in the pot
came out with a splash, all over her!
There was jam on her whiskers, and jam
behind her ears, jam on her pink nose,
jam on her face, jam on her tail—
jam all over her!
She was in such a sticky mess
that she couldn't move.
So there she had to stay
until twelve o'clock.

When the other mice came at twelve
o'clock, they licked her clean!

Next morning the old woman
came down to work in her kitchen.
She found one of the jam pots
over on its side, but she couldn't think
where all the jam had gone.

But the wee white mice knew!

Manu and the Fish

This story is very old. It is as old as
the high mountains of India.
It is so old that men told it when the
greatest river in all India was only
a tiny stream.

★ ★ ★ ★ ★ ★

Once there was a good and kind man
called Manu. He lived alone in a
little hut by the banks of a river.
One morning he took a large jug and
went down to the river to wash.
He dipped the jug in the pool where
the water ran clear and clean.

As he lifted the jug something flashed,
bright and silver, in the bottom.
It was a small fish. Manu was about to
tip it back into the river again,
when suddenly the fish spoke to him.

"Master," it said. "Please, I beg you,

don't put me back into the river.
I'm so small, and the larger fish
will eat me."

Manu was amazed.

"Tell me what I must do, little fish,"
he said. "And I'll help you if I can."

"You must keep me in this jug,"
said the fish, "until I'm as long as
your hand. Then you must dig
a hole beside your hut and fill it
with water from the river.
There you will keep me until I'm
as long as your arm."

"And what then, little fish?" asked Manu.

"Then you may put me back into
the river, for I will be able to
take care of myself."

Manu did as he was told. At first
the little fish lived in the jug and
Manu kept its water clean and fresh.
The fish grew bigger, and as it grew
its colour changed. It turned from silver

to gold and scarlet and green. It looked
as if a rainbow had fallen into Manu's
old jug. As it grew, a strange silver
horn started to grow on its head.
It was a very fine fish indeed.

At last the day came when the

little fish was as long as Manu's hand.
For three days Manu dug until
he had made a deep hole in the earth
beside his hut. He put stones in the
bottom of the hole to make cool places
where a little fish might lie
in the heat of the day. Then Manu
filled the hole with water from the river,
and the little fish swam happily
in its new home.

The little fish grew bigger and the
silver horn on its head grew stronger.
For many years Manu and the fish
lived together very happily as friends.

Then at last came a time when the
fish was as long as Manu's arm.

"You must take me to the river,"
said the fish, "and leave me there."

Manu did what he was told,
though he was sad to lose his friend.
But every day when he went to the river
to wash, the fish came back to talk to him.

One morning the fish came with a warning.

"There will be a great flood," it said. "And the water will cover all the land. You have been my friend, so I will help you."

"What must I do?" asked Manu.

"You must build a boat," said the fish.

"It must be a strong boat that will float on the floods. Into it you must take the wisest men you know, and the seeds of all the plants you can find."

So Manu built a boat. He cut trees from the forest and tied them together to make a raft. On top of the raft he made a little hut.
Into the hut he put jugs and bowls with the seeds of all the plants that he

could find.

Then Manu went to the wise men and told them what the fish had said.
The wisest of them listened to Manu and went with him on his raft.

And so came the heavy rains of India.
The little streams grew into rivers,
and the rivers grew and spread into lakes.
The whole land was covered with water.
Only the top of the highest mountain in

all India was still to be seen.

Manu and the wise men sat in the little hut on the raft. They heard the rain beating on the roof and the wind blowing. They were tossed here and there by the wild waves.

Then the fish came again to Manu.

"Tie a rope to the raft," it said, "and throw the other end over my horn." The fish pulled them to the high mountain which stood like a little island above the floods. Manu tied the boat safely to a rock.

It happened as the fish had said. The rains stopped and the sun shone again. Each day the floods fell a little lower. The boat floated back down to the bottom of the mountain. At last, after many weeks, the waters dried up and the boat was left sitting on the plain of rich, wet earth.

Manu and the wise men came out into the sunshine. They took the pots of seeds and planted them all around. Each year the plants grew and spread more seeds. At last the whole of India was filled once more with their colours and sweet-smelling flowers.

Adapted by Moira Miller

Little Sand Horse

An old, old man sat on the sea shore.
He was too old to swim,
and too old to make sand castles
or dig holes.

He was too old to find shells,
or to play with seaweed, so he just sat
and drew with a stick on the sand.
He drew a starfish and a boat,
then rubbed them out. He drew a monkey
and a tiny dog, then rubbed them out.

He drew a cow and a pig,
and then rubbed them out.
He drew a little horse with a funny nose
and a waving tail.

Then he laughed to himself,
for it seemed as if the horse had
winked at him.

The sun was sinking over the sea,
and the air was growing cold.
The grown-ups took their bags.
The children left their sand castles.
They all went away from the beach,
until at last the old man was alone.
Then he too thought of home.
He bent down to rub away the horse
he had drawn on the sand, but again
it seemed as if it winked at him.
He smiled and said,

"Very well, Little Sand Horse,
I'll leave you for the tide to wash away.
Then you can go with the children's
castles and sand pies, their deep holes

and their motor cars of sand—
far out to sea.
Goodnight, Little Sand Horse.
You'll go with the tide tonight."

The old man went slowly, slowly
across the beach and up the hill.

Little Sand Horse waited.
The sea rose higher and higher,
and came nearer and nearer.
It washed away the castles and the
sand pies. It filled up the holes.
It took back a jelly fish
and some green seaweed.

Little Sand Horse waited. He knew
that when the waves touched him he would
come to life. He made up his mind
that he would not go out to sea.
He would run up the beach
and have one night of fun.
The sea rose higher and higher,
and came nearer and nearer, splashing
in silver waves on the beach.

Little Sand Horse waited and waited.
Then the tip of a wave touched him.
He found he could move—his legs,
his tail, and then his body.

A larger wave washed right over him.
Little Sand Horse jumped up and tried
to run away, but he wasn't quick enough.
Another big wave rushed on to him
and tried to wash him out to sea.
He splashed and splashed, and was able
to keep up. When the next wave
went rushing on to the beach
Little Sand Horse went with it.
He jumped quickly out of its way
before it could take him back again.
He ran up the beach on to the dry sand.
Then he shook the water from his eyes,
and laughed at the rising moon.

Little Sand Horse knew
what he wanted to do first of all.
When he was lying on the sand
beside the old man, he had seen,

a little way off, swings and see-saws,
where children were playing.
It was still light enough to see,
and he ran to a swing. He sat on it
and sailed up and down through the air
until it grew dark.
The stars twinkled down at him
and the moon shone
like a great silver ball in the sky.

Little Sand Horse thought he would try
a see-saw next. He ran over the sand
and soon found a see-saw.

He sat on the end that was down,
and waited happily for it to take him up,
but of course it didn't move.

"That's funny," said Sand Horse
to himself. "The children went up and
down all the time. I saw them as I lay
on the sand. I want to go up!"
He started walking along the see-saw
to the "Up" end, but before he reached it,
it had gone down with a bang.

"Bother!" said Little Sand Horse,
and he started walking back again.
But before he reached the first end,
that, too, had gone down with a bang.
So he went on, scrambling quickly from
one end to the other end of the see-saw,
but he couldn't make himself go up.

Then he heard a little laugh.

"You want me on there with you,"
said a voice, and looking down, Sand Horse
saw a small toy rabbit.

"Sit still," said the rabbit, and

he climbed on to the end of the see-saw.
Up went Sand Horse in the air.

"Oo oo oo!" he cried. "This is fine!"
The two little friends played
on the see-saw until they were tired.
By that time they had talked a lot,
and laughed a lot,
and were very good friends.

"Tell me," said Sand Horse as they went
off together. "How did you come here?"

"My name is Blink," replied the rabbit.
"I'm really a toy, but Pat, the little
girl who owns me, forgot about me today.
She left me on the sands.
When the waves tried
to wash me out to sea, I came to life.
I ran away from them
because I wanted one night of fun."

"Like me," said Sand Horse,
and he told Blink his story.
"I got up and ran away
from the rushing waves too,

because I wanted one night of fun.
So here we are together.
Where shall we go now?"

"I know," replied Blink,
"the ice-cream stall! I've been
carried past it often. I've seen
so many people eating ices that I've
longed and longed for one, but no one
ever thought of buying one for me."

The ice-cream stall was locked, but
the animals were able to pull a window
open, and Blink went in.

"Hurry," whispered Little Sand Horse
after a while, but at that moment
out came Blink, holding a big ice cream
in each hand. They went on, licking
their ice creams. Little Sand Horse
was as happy as he could be.

Soon they came to a roundabout.
They stopped to look.
It had twelve bright wooden horses
standing half asleep in a ring.

"Want a go?" asked Blink.
"I've been on it with Pat.
I'll turn the handle for you."

Little Sand Horse was too happy
to speak as he climbed on to one
of the wooden horses. Blink turned
the handle, and round spun Sand Horse,
round and round and round.

"That was fine!" he said, as he jumped to the ground again.

The Roundabout Horse looked at him and asked,

"How would you like to spin round like that all day?"

"It would be lovely," replied Sand Horse.

"Well, change places with me and give me a holiday. I'll come back tomorrow night. Will you?"

"Y-yes." Little Sand Horse climbed up into the wooden horse's place on the roundabout. The wooden horse jumped down beside Blink.
Blink looked up at his friend.

"Little Sand Horse, I don't think you'll like it," he said. Just then there was a red glow in the sky.

"That's the sun getting up," cried Blink. "We must hurry. Goodbye."
Away he ran with Roundabout Horse,

but Roundabout Horse found it hard
to go straight. He could only run round
and round, and that took a long time.

★ ★ ★ ★ ★ ★

At nine o'clock in the morning
the Roundabout Man came. He looked
at Little Sand Horse, and said,
"This horse looks different today."
Then he shouted, "Roundabout!
Roundabout! Ten pence a go!"
A lot of children came and
took their seats on the horses. He
turned the handle, and away they went,
round and round and round.
Little Sand Horse thought it was grand,
although he was carrying
a little boy on his back.
When those children had finished,
more came, and then still more.

Little Sand Horse began to feel sick.
He was so giddy that even when

the roundabout was still, his poor head
seemed to go round just the same.
He never wanted to ride again,
but he had to do it, all day long.

"Oh, for the nice cool sand
and the sea," he sighed.

"Roundabout! Ten pence a go!"
cried the Roundabout Man.

"Roundabout! Ten pence a go!"
Along came more and more children.
Little Sand Horse felt a little girl
climb on his back, and to his joy
he saw that she held a toy rabbit,
and the rabbit was Blink!

"Hello," whispered Blink.
"How do you like it?"

"Oh!" sighed Little Sand Horse.
"Round and round, all day long!
I can't bear it."

"Never mind," went on Blink. "Tonight
there's a party for lost toys and sand people,
at the bottom of the sea. Shall we go?"

Little Sand Horse nodded.

"But do you think Roundabout Horse will come back here tonight?"

Blink smiled. "Poor Roundabout Horse! He can't walk straight, and he's lying in a hut.
He's longing for tonight, so that he can get back to his roundabout."

"And you?" asked Little Sand Horse.
"How will you come?"

"I'll slip out of Pat's hand, and stay behind on the beach till it's dark."

The roundabout stopped. Pat jumped down, and she and Blink went away. Little Sand Horse waited and waited. Evening came. The children went home to bed. The Roundabout Man mopped his hot face, and went home too.

It was dark. The stars twinkled, and the moon shone like a great silver ball. Little Sand Horse waited and waited and waited.
Where was Blink? Would he be able to get away? Perhaps Roundabout Horse wouldn't come back.

"Ah!" Then he sighed with joy, for there, coming towards him, was Blink, with poor old Roundabout Horse trying to walk straight.
The wooden horse was so pleased

to get back that he almost pushed
Little Sand Horse out of his way.
He took his place once more on the
roundabout, and looked very happy.

"I'll give you a ride before I go,"
said kind Blink, and he turned the handle.
Round and round went Roundabout Horse.

"Thank you, Blink," he said. "I feel
better now." But Little Sand Horse
was not so happy. He found that he
was walking round and round,
and it was very hard to go straight.

"Come on," he said, and they called
goodbye to Roundabout Horse,
who was going round and round,
waving his tail.

They walked down to the beach.

"Sand!" cried Little Sand Horse,
and he jumped with joy. Then he thought
of the party. "Blink," he said,
"if we go to the bottom of the sea,
we'll have to stay there, you know.

I'll be glad, but wouldn't you rather
go back to Pat?" Blink shook his head.

"No," he said. "She has lots of toys.
Besides, I'd rather come with you."
He found a long piece
of green seaweed and put it round
Little Sand Horse's neck.
Then he jumped on his back.

"Come, Little Sand Horse," he cried,
"or we'll be late for the party."

So Little Sand Horse splashed into
the cold waves. Blink pulled at the
seaweed, and together they sailed
far away on the splashing waters,
away and away, and out to sea.

The Coal Lorry

There was once a coalman
who was driving his lorry
through a quiet little village.
The lorry was an open one
with twenty sacks of coal on it.

Suddenly the lorry skidded.
The wheels slipped and slid.
The sacks of coal rattled and shook.
The coalman tried hard
to get the lorry straight again,
but it slid across the road,
it slid across the path,
and it crashed into a wall!
Crash! Bang! Rattle!

Some of the sacks tipped over
on to their sides,

and the coal slid slowly out.
Some of the sacks fell to the ground
and burst open with a bang.
Crash! Bang! Rattle! Out fell the coal,
big lumps, little lumps,
black and shining.
Coal fell on the road.
Coal fell on the path.
Coal fell everywhere!

The coalman put on the brakes
and jumped down.

"It's lucky I'm not hurt," he thought,
"and it's lucky there is no one about."
He looked round.
The lorry had a big dent in the front.
The wall had lost a few bricks.
There was coal on the road.
There was coal on the path.
There was coal everywhere,
big lumps, little lumps,
black and shining.

"I'll phone the coal office,"

thought the coalman, and he walked away
up the road to the phone box.

Just then some children came along
on their way home from school.

"Look!" they cried to each other.
They stared at the lorry
with the dent in front.
They stared at the wall
with the missing bricks.
They stared at the coal,
big lumps, little lumps,
black and shining.

Now the children had always been told
to keep their village clean and tidy.
They never dropped bits of paper
on the path, and if they found any,
they quickly put them in a litter bin.
So, after a moment one child said,

"We'd better clear up the mess."
Some children ran home
to fetch toy carts and wheelbarrows
and boxes on wheels.

Some ran home to fetch old prams
and buckets and baskets and bags.

In a few minutes the boys and girls
were all picking up coal.
Some of them dug it up with spades.
Some of them picked up the lumps
one by one. They filled their toy carts
and wheelbarrows and boxes on wheels.
They filled their old prams and buckets
and baskets and bags,
and ran home with their loads.
Then they emptied the coal
into their own coal sheds
and ran back to the lorry
to get some more.

More children came along
and began to help.
Some grown-ups heard the news
and came to help too.

They were all very proud
of their clean, tidy village,
and in a short time

they had cleared all the coal away.
Then the baker brought along a broom
and swept the road and the path clean.
Not a single lump of coal
was left on the road.
Not a single lump of coal
was left on the path.
There was not even a speck of coal dust
to be seen.

The coalman was in the phone box
a long time because he couldn't get
the right number.
Then at last he spoke to someone
at the coal office and walked slowly
back to his lorry.

"Now I'll have to put all the coal
back into the sacks," he thought.
"What a job that will be."
He saw a crowd of people
standing round the lorry,
but where was the coal?
Not a single lump of coal
was left on the road.
Not a single lump of coal
was left on the path.
There was not even a speck of coal dust
to be seen.

The coalman went up to the people
who were standing round the lorry.
They were all looking very pleased
with themselves.

"My coal!" said the coalman.
"Where's my coal?"

"We cleared it all up for you,"
said one of the children.

"But where is it?" asked the coalman.
"I must have it back.
There was fifty pounds' worth
of coal there!"

"That's right,"
added the village policeman,
who had just appeared.
"Where *is* his coal?"

Everyone looked surprised,
and the children began to feel worried.

"Have *you* any of the coal?"
the policeman said sternly to the boy
who was standing nearest to him.

"Yes," replied the boy.

"How much?" asked the policeman.

"Six toy carts full," said the boy.

"And you?" said the policeman
to a girl.

"I took some home in our old pram,"
she whispered.
Oh dear! The children had tried so hard
to keep the village clean and tidy.
Even the grown-ups
had not stopped to think
that they were all really stealing.

"The coal will have to be
given back," said the policeman,
"every single lump of it."

So the children went home
to bring back the coal they had taken.
They filled up their toy carts
and wheelbarrows and boxes on wheels.
They filled up their old prams
and buckets and baskets and bags.
They took all the coal back
to the coalman, and they helped him
to fill up his sacks again.
They gave back all the big lumps,
all the little lumps,
all the black and shining coal.

The Tortoise Who Talked too Much

Once upon a time, far away,
there was a pool of water.
At the edge of it grew tall reeds
and bright little flowers.

One summer, a tortoise made his home
in the stones on the bank,
and two geese built a nest
among the reeds and grasses.
They all became good friends.

The geese swam on the pond,
and flew over the hills. The tortoise

nibbled the grass, and cooled himself
in the mud. Often in the evenings
they told stories to each other.
The geese told of the things they saw
when they flew over the hills. Tortoise
made up stories to tell. They were
very good stories, but they were
always too long.

They went on, and on, and on.
Sometimes they went on so long
that the geese grew sleepy
and closed their eyes.

"He's a nice tortoise,"
the first goose would say
when they were alone.

"Yes, if only he didn't talk so much,"
said the second goose.

But nothing ever seemed
to stop Tortoise. He talked and talked.

Every day the sun shone.
It was very hot. The pool began to get
dry at the edges. It grew smaller
and smaller. Soon it was so small
that there was not enough water
for the geese to swim upon.
Then it was so small that there was
not enough water for them to drink.

"We must fly away," said the geese
at last, "and find another pool.
There isn't enough water left here."

"We are sorry to leave you,"
they told Tortoise, "but we must go
tomorrow."

"Oh, don't leave me," begged Tortoise.

"I don't want to stay here alone. There will be no one to talk to me."

"We are sorry," said the geese. "We must go. We must fly over the hills, and find another pool."

"Don't leave me," cried Tortoise again. "Take me with you."

"We can't do that," said the geese. "You have no wings. You can't fly."

"No," said Tortoise sadly. "I have no wings. I can't fly." He went on talking. He said how lonely it would be without the geese. He said how lucky they were to have wings. He talked and talked and talked. Suddenly he said,

"I know! I have a plan!"

"What is it?"

"You two can fly close together, holding a stick in your beaks. I can hang on to the middle of the stick with my mouth. In that way you can take me with you through the air."

The geese were still for a moment.
Then the first one said,
"It's a good plan."
"Yes," said the second,
"but it won't work."
"Why not?" asked Tortoise.
"Because you talk too much.
If you say even one word,
you'll let go of the stick.
Then you'll fall."
"Oh! But I can be quiet. I know I can.
I won't talk at all. I won't say
one word."
"Are you sure?" said the geese.
"Quite sure," said Tortoise.
"Very well. Then we'll take you."

Next morning the geese found a stick,
not too long and not too short,
not too thick and not too thin.
They stood close together,
and held it in their beaks.

"Now, Tortoise," they said,
"are you sure you can be quiet?"

"Yes. I won't say one word."
He took hold of the stick with his mouth.
He waved a foot
to show that he was ready.

The two geese went up in the air.
Tortoise went up with them.
The two geese flapped their wings,
and flew over the hill. Tortoise flew
over the hill with them.

He held the stick with his mouth.
He didn't say a word.

Soon the geese flew over a town.
Tortoise saw children playing
on the streets below. The children
looked up and saw him.
They began to laugh.

"Oh, look!" they cried. "Look at the
tortoise flying through the air!
Doesn't he look funny?"

"You look just as funny yourselves!"
said Tortoise crossly.

But oh, dear! He had opened his mouth.
He had let go of the stick!
He was falling, falling, falling!

He was lucky. He fell on some grass,
soft and green, in a garden.
A little girl found him
and made a pet of him.

The geese could not stop. It wasn't
safe for them to land in a town.
They flew on, over the town,

over the hills,
till they found a new pool.
At the edge of it grew tall reeds
and bright little flowers.
The geese built a new nest
among the reeds and grasses.

"Poor Tortoise," said the first goose,
"I wonder what has happened to him."

"He would have been here with us,"
said the second goose, "if only
he hadn't talked so much."

Adapted

Nothing Ever Happens!

Rupindar and her friends were walking home from school together.

Anne-Marie was walking along the top of a wall. She held her arms out like a circus acrobat.

"Can you come round to my house tonight?" she said. "My brother Dave bought me a new game on Saturday. It's great."

"O.K." said Susan and Mandy together.

"I can't come," said Rupindar.
"I've got to go to the shop tonight
and help fill up the shelves."

"What about your brother?" said Susan.
"Doesn't he ever help?"

"Adnan always puts things in the
wrong places," said Rupindar. "I think
he does it on purpose!"

"You're lucky!" said Mandy.
"I'd like to work in a shop like
your Dad's. Imagine—all those sweets!"

"You wouldn't really," said Rupindar.
"It's very boring. Nothing ever happens."

"It would if Mandy was there,"
giggled Anne-Marie. "She'd eat so much
she wouldn't be able to get out of
the door again!"

Mandy pushed Anne-Marie off the wall
and they all laughed.

"I must hurry," said Rupindar.
"I promised I'd go straight from school."

"I'll walk round with you," said Susan,

"and we can do our homework together
in the back. You can help me
with the Maths."

In the shop, Rupindar's Mum was already
filling up the shelves.
She turned and smiled at them.
Her Dad was behind the counter
counting the cash from the till.
So Susan and Rupindar went through the
curtain door into the back shop.
They spread their books on a corner
of the table and Rupindar
went to get some biscuits.
Her Dad came through from the shop.

"Before you start," he said,
"would you like to check this money
for me and make sure it's right?"
He put a bag of ten pence pieces on
the table.

"We'll count them into pounds,"
said Susan, and she tipped out the coins.

"One, two, three, four, five, six,

seven, eight, nine, ten." They started
to count the money and put it into piles.

"That's a funny-looking one," said
Rupindar, lifting out one of the coins.
It was badly bent, and dented
round the edge as though someone had
tried to break it.

"It's all right," said her Dad.
"The bank will take it. Put it in
with the others."

The girls finished counting and handed
the bag back. Rupindar brought two glasses
of orange squash, and they settled down at
the table with their books.

They had been working quietly for a little while when suddenly there was a noise in the shop. Rupindar had heard the bell above the door ring. She knew that someone had just come in.

"Drop it!" she heard a man shout. "And don't try anything funny."

Rupindar and Susan looked at each other.

"Shhh," said Rupindar and tiptoed

over to the door. Through the curtain
she saw a man with a gun standing
in the shop. Another young man
had come round behind the counter and
taken the bag of money from the till.
Rupindar's father was standing with
an arm round her mother, watching them.

"Phone the police!" whispered Susan.

"Can't," hissed Rupindar. "They'd

hear me through the curtain."

She watched as the man behind the counter stuffed all the money into a large bag.

"Is that all?" he snarled. His voice sounded strange. Like the other thief, he was wearing a mask.

"That's the lot," said Rupindar's father. "There isn't any more."

The young man pulled out the drawers behind the counter and tipped everything on to the floor.

"Come on!" said the other one, waving the gun. "That's all there is. Let's go!"

"Do you think that's a real gun?" whispered Susan.

"Shhhhh!" said Rupindar. The man behind the counter sat on it and swung his legs over to the other side. Rupindar saw his feet clearly. The shoes were blue and white. One had a white lace. The other lace

was dark blue, as if it had been
taken from another shoe.

The bell rang again as the door opened
and slammed shut behind the
young men. Rupindar's father rushed
through to the back room
to phone the police.

The detective who came round sat and
listened and took notes. He asked
if any of them could describe
the young men.

"They wore masks," said Rupindar's Dad. "Who knows what they looked like. They were young and wore jeans and anoraks."

"Not much help," said the detective. "A lot of people look like that."

He turned to Rupindar and Susan.

"Don't suppose you two saw anything," he said. "You were both in here, weren't you?"

"I saw his feet," said Rupindar, "the one who took the money." She told the detective about the blue and white shoes with the different coloured laces.

"That's worth looking for," he said. "Anything else you can think of? Pity they were all coins. We could maybe trace pound notes."

"The ten pence piece!" said Susan. They all stared at her.

"It was bent—with the marks round the

edge," she said. "You remember!"

"It's an idea," said the detective. "We'll keep a look out for anyone trying to hand one over."
He put his notebook in his pocket and then stood up.

"You wouldn't like to come with me in the car?" he said. "Just drive round a few cafés? You never know, we might just spot them."

Rupindar and Susan went with the detective. They drove slowly round the dark streets, past shops and cafés, looking in the lighted windows.

An hour later, down a dark side street, they stopped outside a small café. The detective went in to buy some sweets for Rupindar and Susan. In the corner a young man sat with his feet on a chair watching him. Another was playing with a space invaders machine. He stopped, and thumped the machine.

"Give me another ten pence," he said, turning to his friend.

"That one's got stuck in the machine.

It was bent or something."

The detective turned to look at them.
The young man with his feet on the chair
was wearing blue and white shoes.
One of the shoes had a white lace,
the other had a blue lace.

There was no doubt about it.
These men were the ones who had been
in the shop. He walked slowly back
out to the car and over his radio called
for more police. Within minutes
the two thieves were in the back of
a van on their way to the police station.

Rupindar's brother Adnan was
quite annoyed when he came home that
night.

"I missed all the fun," he moaned.
"Nothing ever happens when
I'm here."

"Maybe that's because you're never here!"
laughed Rupindar.

Moira Miller

Martin and the Bear

Many years ago there lived an old man
and an old woman. They had two sons.
The names of the sons were Martin
and Gregor. Gregor was sad and gloomy.
He never smiled when he was talking,
and he never sang when he was working.
All he did was to look gloomy
and to puff away at his pipe
—puff, puff, puff. So people
called him Gregor the gloomy one.

But Martin was very merry and happy.
He laughed when he was talking,
and he sang when he was working. All day
he was merry and bright. So people
called him Martin the merry one.

At night Martin played his fiddle.
As soon as the people heard him,
they wanted to dance.
They could not keep their feet still,
and away they went, dance, dance, dance

to Martin's fiddle.

The old man and the old woman lived with Martin the merry one and Gregor the gloomy one, near a large forest. Near the large forest there was a large lake. Some days Martin would fish in the lake, and Gregor would cut down trees in the forest. On other days Gregor would fish in the lake, and Martin would cut pine logs for firewood.

One day Gregor the gloomy one
got ready to go to the forest.
He took out the sledge, and led
the horse from its stable, for the horse
was to draw the sledge over the snow.
Gregor put his axe in the sledge
and then lit his pipe.
The air was very still.
As Gregor puffed at his pipe,
the smoke went up into the air in rings.

"Gee up!" shouted Gregor as he sat
in the sledge. The horse pulled the
sledge quickly over the white snow.
Soon they came to the forest.
All the fir trees and pine trees
had snow on their branches. The sun
shone down, and made the snow
on the branches sparkle like stars.

At last Gregor stopped his sledge
and jumped out. He took his axe,
and looked for the largest tree
in the forest. Then he saw a tall pine

tree which looked so beautiful with snow
on its branches right up to the top.
Gregor began to cut it down.

"Crack, crack!" went the axe.

"Plop, plop!" went the snow,
as it fell from the branches
each time Gregor hit the tree.

"Snip, snip!" went the chips of wood,
as they fell to the ground
with each stroke of the axe.
What a noise Gregor made as he cut down
the tall pine tree! The air was so still
that you could hear the noise
all over the forest.

Now, not far away there lived
a brown bear. The noise woke the bear,
and he called out,

"Who's making that noise?
Who's cutting down the trees
in this forest?"

As the bear came along in the snow,
he saw Gregor, and he growled,

"You're making a lot of noise.
You woke me with your crack, crack,
your plop, plop, and your snip, snip.
I want to sleep, and you won't let me."

But Gregor the gloomy one didn't say a word. So the bear growled again,

"You can't chop down those pine trees. You can't smoke your pipe in my forest. You're spoiling the air with the smoke from your pipe."

But still Gregor didn't say a word. He went on cutting down the tree and puffing away at his pipe. Just then a great heap of snow fell from one of the branches right on top of the bear.

"Stop!" growled the bear,
but still Gregor went on chopping.

By this time the bear was really very angry, and he took hold of Gregor by the arm. Gregor dropped his axe, and rolled over and over in the snow with the bear. They did look funny

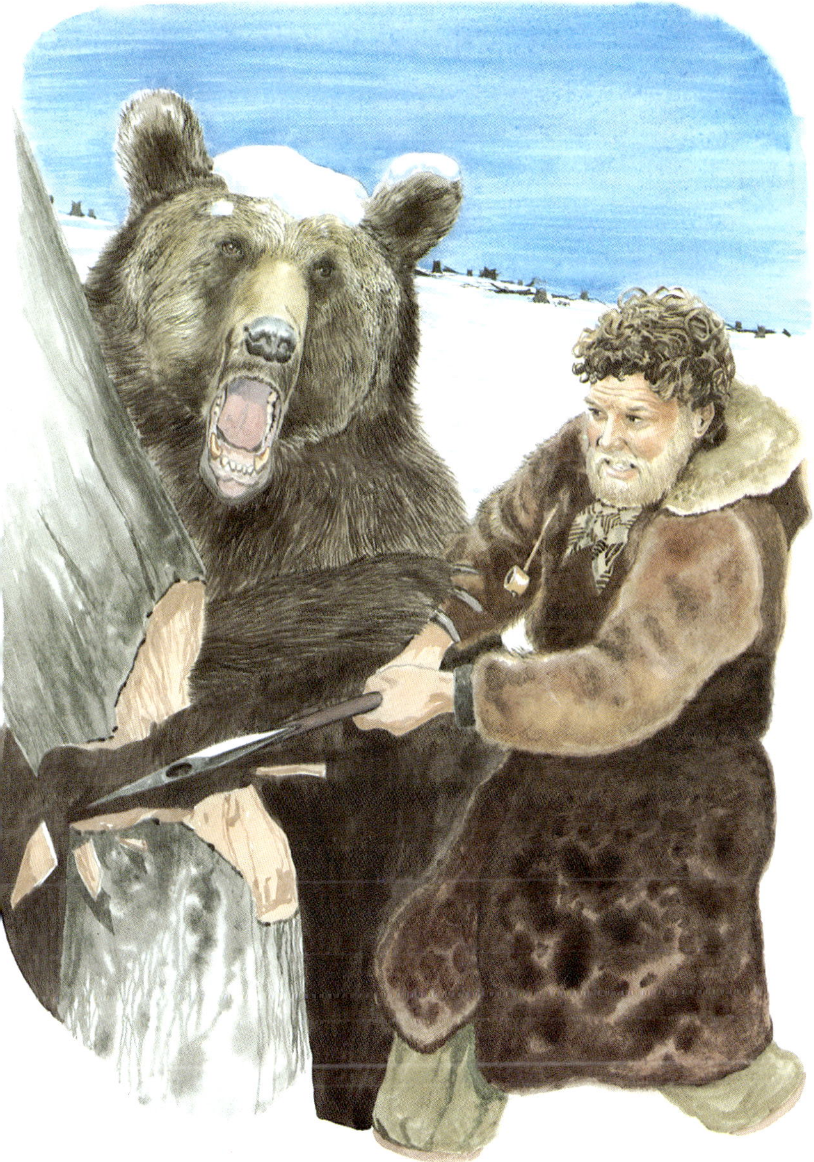

kicking up the snow as they rolled
over and over. First you would see
the bear's leg, then Gregor's arm, then
his head, then the bear's head, as they
rolled together in the white snow.

As they came near the sledge, Gregor
fell into it. The horse started
to move, and away it went.
Gregor was on the sledge all right,
but without his axe or his pipe
or his fur cap. Then the horse went
over the snow to Gregor's log house,
until the bear and the forest were left
far behind.

When the sledge stopped outside the
log house, Gregor's father and mother
came out and saw him covered with snow.

"Gregor, where have you been?
Where is the pine wood for the fire,
and where are your axe, your pipe,
and your fur cap?" they asked.

So Gregor told them about the fight.

The people came out and stood around.
They heard all about the bear
that didn't like the noise or the smoke.

Just then Martin came home from
the lake with some fish. But there was
no wood to put on the fire to cook
the fish. So Martin said,

"I must go to the forest to get some
wood." He took his axe, and put it
on the sledge. He also took his fiddle.
He drove the sledge over the snow
to the forest. He stopped the horse
just by the tree that Gregor had been
cutting. He saw chips all around
on the ground. He saw Gregor's axe
and his fur cap near by.

"Oh," said Martin. "So this is where
Gregor met the bear." He sat down for
a while and began to think.

"The bear doesn't like noise and he
doesn't like smoke. I wonder if he likes
a fiddle. I think I'll play a tune

before I cut some firewood."

So Martin took his fiddle from the sledge, and began to play a dance tune. The air was so still that you could hear the tune all over the forest.
It woke up the bear.

"What's that?" said the bear to himself. "I like that tune. It makes me want to dance." So the bear ran along in the snow to where Martin was playing his fiddle. As the bear drew near Martin, he began to dance.

He kicked up the snow in the air
as he danced. He puffed and he grunted
as he went round and round. Martin
played faster and faster, and the bear
went faster and faster, until he could
dance no more.

"Stop, stop!" shouted the bear.

Martin stopped playing,
and the bear came up to him.

"Will you teach me
to play the fiddle?" said the bear.
"I want to teach my cubs to dance."

"Yes. Yes. I will," said Martin.
"Just watch me, and then you do
what I am doing." Martin played a little
tune. Then the bear took the fiddle.
He pushed the bow across the strings,
but what a noise he made—squeak,
squeak, squang, squang. His paws were
too big, and his claws were too long.
As he pushed the bow across the fiddle,
his claws caught in the strings.

"Oh! Oh!" shouted Martin. "That's no
good. It's not much like a dance
tune. Your claws are too long, and your
paws are too thick. You must have your
paws made thinner. Come this way
with me."

Martin led the bear to a big pine tree.
He split open the pine tree with his axe,
and then said to the bear,

"Put your paws in this crack."
The bear put his paws in the crack.
Then Martin took out the axe, so that

the bear's paws were squeezed a little.

"Oh! Oh!" shouted the bear. "My paws are squeezed so that I can't take them out of this crack."

"That's to make your paws thinner and your claws shorter," said Martin. "You'll be able to play the fiddle then, and teach your cubs to dance."

"I don't want to play the fiddle," roared the bear. "Let me out! Let me out! I don't want my paws made thinner, or my claws made shorter. I don't want to teach my cubs to dance."

"I'll let you out," said Martin, "if you'll let the people come into the forest to get firewood."

"Yes, yes," roared the bear. "I'll let the people come into the forest to cut down the pine trees for firewood. Let me out! Let me out!"

When Martin opened the crack in the tree, the brown bear took

his paws out, and away he ran, over
the snow to his den. So Martin cut down
the pine tree and split it into logs
for firewood. Then he put the logs
on the sledge and drove home.

When the people heard Martin,
they came out and stood around.

"How did you get all these logs?"
they asked. "Didn't the bear
drive you away?"

"Oh, no," said Martin. "I played
on my fiddle, and the bear danced
till he could dance no more.
Then he wanted to play the fiddle."

The people laughed when Martin told
them about the noise the bear made
when he tried to play the fiddle.
He told them also how the bear roared
when his paws were squeezed in a pine
tree. Again the people laughed.

"And," said Martin, "I let him out
only when he promised to let us go

to the forest to get firewood."

The people shouted for joy, and cried, "Play us a tune on your fiddle! Play us a dance tune." Martin played a tune, and the people danced. They sang and danced to merry Martin's tune, until night came and the white snow began to fall.

The Fisherman
and His Wife

There was once a poor fisherman
who lived with his wife
in a shabby little hut near the sea.

One day as he sat on the shore, fishing,
he felt a strong tug on his line.

"This feels like a very big fish,"
he thought, and he pulled and pulled,
and out of the water came a great fish!

"Oh please let me go," cried the fish.
"I'm not really a fish at all.
I'm an enchanted prince."

"Of course I'll let you go,"
replied the fisherman. "I don't want

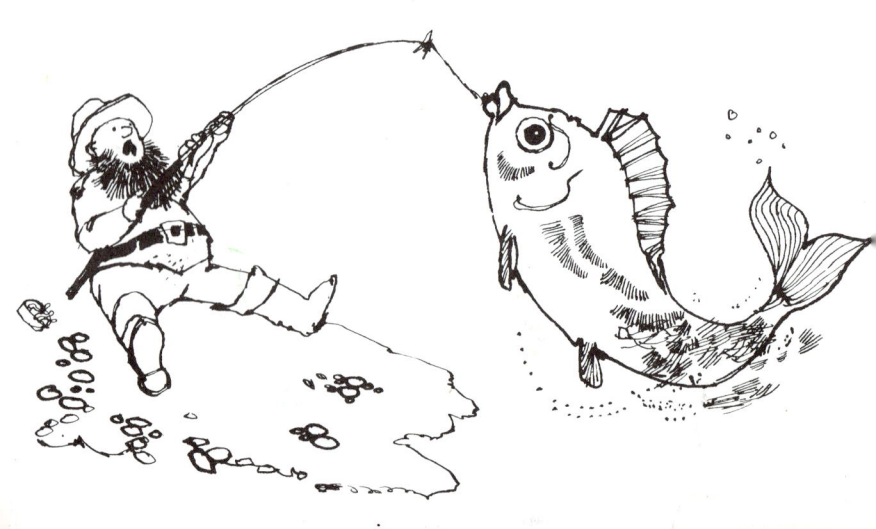

anything to do with a fish
that can talk."

So he put the great fish back
in the clear water, and watched it swim
deep down below.

When the fisherman returned home,
his wife said,

"Didn't you catch anything today?"

"No," replied the fisherman.
"Well, I did catch a fish but it said
it was really an enchanted prince
and it asked me to let it go.
So I put it back in the water."

"Didn't you ask it
to give you anything
before you set it free?" said the wife.

"No," replied the fisherman.
"What should I have asked it for?"

"Oh, you are stupid," said the wife.
"Go back and say we would like
a nice cottage instead of this shabby
little hut."

The fisherman didn't like the idea of
asking for anything, but he went back
to the seashore.

The water was not so clear now. It was
a strange green and yellow colour.
The fisherman called out to the fish
and it came swimming at once
to the top of the water.

"What do you want?" asked the fish.

"My wife said I should have asked you
for something before I set you free.
She is tired of living in our shabby
little hut.
She would like a nice cottage instead,"
said the fisherman.

"Go home," said the fish.
"She has it already."

So the fisherman went home, and there
instead of the shabby little hut,
he saw a beautiful little cottage.
His wife stood at the door
and took him inside.

"There!" she said. "Isn't this much better than the shabby little hut?"

In the cottage was a bedroom, a living room and a kitchen. There were beds and a cupboard in the bedroom. There were chairs and a table in the living room. There were pots and pans and plates and cups in the kitchen.

In a yard at the back there were hens and ducks. There was also a small garden, full of flowers and vegetables and fruit.

"How nice it all is!" said the fisherman. "Now we shall be really happy."

For two weeks all went well.
Then the fisherman's wife said crossly,

"This cottage is too small for us,
and the garden isn't big enough.
I'd like to live in a big stone castle.
Go back to the fish and ask it
to give us a castle."

"Oh, I don't like to do that,"
replied the fisherman. "This cottage
is good enough for us. We can't ask
the fish for anything else."

"Yes, we can," said the wife. "Go on.
Go and ask for a big stone castle."

So the fisherman went out,
but his heart was heavy.

"It isn't right to ask the fish
for that," he thought.

When he came to the sea,
it was no longer green and yellow.
It was dark blue and mauve.
The fisherman called to the fish
and it came swimming at once

to the top of the water.

"What do you want?" it asked.

"My wife is tired of the cottage,"
replied the fisherman sadly.
"She told me to ask you to give us
a big stone castle instead."

"Go home," said the fish.
"She has it already."

So the fisherman went home, and there,
instead of the cottage,
he saw a big stone castle.
His wife stood at the door
and took him inside.

"There!" she said. "Isn't this
much better than the little cottage?"

The fisherman looked round
and could hardly believe his eyes.
There was a great hall of marble,
with lights of crystal hanging
from the ceiling.
There were many, many rooms
with thick, soft carpets on the floors.

There were chairs and tables of gold,
and there were servants standing
at every door.

At the back of the castle
was a large courtyard
with stables full of horses.
There were coaches and coachmen.
There was a beautiful garden, full
of flowers and vegetables and fruit,
and there was a great park, where deer
and goats and sheep and cows fed.

"It's all wonderful!"
said the fisherman. "Now we can live

here happily for the rest of our lives."

"Well, we shall see," replied his wife.

Next morning when the wife awoke,
she looked out of the window
and saw all the land in the distance
outside the castle walls.

She woke the fisherman up and said,

"Come and look at all this land."

"Yes. It is beautiful," he replied.

"I want it all to belong to me,"
said the wife. "Go to the fish and ask it
to make me king of all the land."

"King!" cried the fisherman.
"How could you be king? Even the fish
couldn't make you king."

"Yes, it could," went on the wife.
"Go and ask it."

Sadly the fisherman dressed himself
and went out, but his heart was heavy.

"It isn't right to ask the fish
for that," he thought.

When he came to the sea,

it was dark grey and wild,
and the fisherman was afraid.
He called to the fish
and it came swimming at once
to the top of the water.

"What does she want now?" it asked.

"She wants to be king!" he replied.

"Go home," said the fish.
"She is king already."

So the fisherman went home
and he heard trumpets and bugles,
and he saw rows of soldiers
guarding the castle.

He went inside and there was his wife.
She was sitting on a high throne
made of gold and diamonds.
On her head she wore a great crown
of pure gold, set with shining jewels.
On each side of her stood
six ladies-in-waiting.
Each was a head smaller than the one
next to her.

The fisherman stared at his wife.

"So now you are king?" he said.

"Yes," she replied. "Now I am king."

He stared at her again and said,

"Now there is nothing else
you can wish for."

"We shall see," replied his wife.

That night the fisherman slept well,
for he was tired, but his wife hardly
slept at all. She was so busy
trying to think what to wish for next.

In the morning when the sun rose,
it shone in through the window.

"Ah!" thought the fisherman's wife,
"I will wish to be lord of the sun
and the moon. Then I'll be able
to tell the sun when to rise
and when to set. And I'll be able
to tell the moon when to rise
and when to set."

She pushed her husband with her elbow
and said,

"Wake up. Wake up. Go to the fish and ask it to make me lord of the sun and the moon."

The fisherman was so shocked at the very thought, that he fell out of bed.

"What did you say?" he asked.

"I want to be lord of the sun and the moon," she replied. "I want to tell the sun when to rise and when to set. I want to tell the moon when to rise and when to set. Go on. Go and ask the fish."

"No, no," said the fisherman. "I can't do that."

"Yes, you can," went on his wife. "I am king and you must do what I say! Go and ask the fish to make me lord of the sun and the moon."

"No, no," said the fisherman again. "I can't do that," but he went out all the same.

His heart was heavy, and as he walked,

a great storm arose. The wind was so wild
and strong that he could hardly stand
against it. The sky grew black as pitch.
Lightning flashed and thunder rolled
in the mountains. White foam was tossed
up and down on the dark sea,
and the waves were as high
as the church tower.

The fisherman trembled with fear.
He called to the fish but he could hardly
hear his own voice above the storm.
He shouted to it and it came swimming
at once to the shore.

"What does she want now?" it asked,
and the fisherman could see that it
was very angry.

"She wants—she wants me to ask you
to make her lord of the sun and the moon.
She wants to tell the sun when to rise
and when to set. She wants
to tell the moon when to rise
and when to set."

"Go home," said the fish.
"You will find her in your old hut
again."

So the fisherman went home,
and when he got there,
there was no big stone castle.
There was no little cottage.
There was only the shabby little hut
where he and his wife had lived
in the beginning.
And there they still live to this day.

Adapted

How Maui Caught the Great Sun

This story is about a clever and cunning young man called Maui (say "mow-ee"—*mow* rhymes with *now*).

The story comes from far away, in the beautiful green islands of the Pacific Ocean. The children there are like children anywhere. They love to play games, to fish and to swim. And at the end of a long day they like to sit round the fire listening to a story.

"Which story will it be tonight?" says the story-teller.

"Tell us about Maui!" shout the children. "Tell us again about Maui!"

There are many, many stories about Maui. This is one of the favourites.

★ ★ ★ ★ ★ ★

When the world began and Maui was

young, he lived at home
with all his brothers.
They spent their time hunting or
fishing all day long, and they were
very happy, except for one thing.
The day was so short.

Each morning the Great Sun jumped
from his bed in the Eastern Sea.
Maui and his brothers had only just
wakened up when he was hurrying
across the sky. They had to
rush through their work while there was

still light. There was no time to stop
and eat, or talk to a friend.
There was no time to lie on the beach
or play games. Every short hour of
light had to be used for work
before the Great Sun rushed to
his bed in the Western Sea.

"If only the days were long!" they
moaned. "How much more we could do!"
They begged the Great Sun to slow down,
but he wouldn't listen to them
and thought only of himself.
Maui became very angry.

"This can't go on," he said.
"We must catch the Great Sun and
make the days longer."

His brothers laughed at him.

"And how are you going to do that,
Maui?" they asked. "Will you go fishing
for the Great Sun with your little hook?"

"Not with my hook," said Maui.
"That would be stupid."

His brothers nodded their heads.

"I'll catch him with a rope!" said Maui. "Catch him and keep him."

Maui's brothers laughed until their sides ached. Maui became angry with them.

"You must help me," he shouted. "We must use the strongest ropes you can make."

"Oh Maui," said his oldest brother. "Even the strongest ropes will burn and the Great Sun will scorch us all before we can catch him."

But Maui wouldn't listen. The next day he went out and picked a great heap of long green leaves from the flax plants that grew in the islands. Along with all his brothers and their wives, he wove the leaves into the ropes that would catch the Great Sun. They worked all day and long into the night. At last they had a great heap of strong green rope.

"Now," said Maui, "tomorrow we will
set out to catch the Great Sun.
We must go to the place where he rises
every morning."

Very early the next morning,
Maui and his brothers crept out of
their huts. They gathered up
the heap of rope and each brother
wrapped a coil round himself.
All day, as the Great Sun hurried
across the sky to the place
where he slept in the Western Sea,
Maui and his brothers hurried
to the east. By the time it was dark
they had come to the Edge of Land
by the Eastern Sea, where the Great Sun
would rise in the morning.

"Now we must build a wall," said Maui.
"It will protect us from the heat."

He showed his brothers how to build
a wall of thick clay. At each end
they built a tall tower of tree trunks.

Then Maui took the rope and
in the middle he made a huge loop
with a knot. When he had done that,
he stretched the rope between the towers.

"Now we must wait," he laughed,
and settled down behind the wall.
The brothers held on to the ends of the
rope in each tower. They waited
and waited, all through the night.

In the morning, the Great Sun awoke.
He jumped out of bed and

tripped into the loop.

"*Pull!*" shouted Maui. "Pull for all you are worth!" And his brothers pulled on the ends of the rope. The loop tightened and the Great Sun was trapped.

The Great Sun fought and struggled. He flamed and flashed and roared. But the more he pulled, the tighter the loop became.
The rope stretched and groaned but

the green flax was strong.

"Hold tight!" shouted Maui. "Hold tight!" At the end of the wall the brothers pulled on the rope, and in the middle the Great Sun raged and roared, screaming with anger.

Then Maui took his club and ran along in the shelter of the thick clay wall. He reached up and beat the Great Sun round the head. As the sun roared and tried to catch him, Maui ducked down behind the wall again. Then, jumping up, he beat the sun on the head again.

The battle raged on until at last the Great Sun sank to the ground.

"Stop, stop!" he begged. "Why do you treat me like this?"

"We only want you to do as we ask," shouted Maui from behind the wall. "We have begged you to slow down so that our days will be longer. You wouldn't listen to us so we have caught you.

We won't let you go until you
promise to give us longer light."

"I promise!" sighed the Great Sun.
"I promise. Only please set me free."

"Then we'll let you go," said Maui.
His brothers dropped the ends of
the rope and the loop fell away.

Slowly the Great Sun stretched out
and reached up into the sky.
Maui stood and watched as he crept
higher and higher.

"Not too fast, mind!" shouted Maui.
I'll keep my rope, just in case."

But the Great Sun was afraid of Maui
and he never had to use the rope again.
It still lies where he left it
by the thick clay wall at the Edge of Land.

And from that day to this the Great Sun
still creeps so slowly across the sky
that you can hardly see him move.

Adapted by Moira Miller

Lucky Hans

Hans worked for seven years.
Then he said to his master,
"I should like to go home now,
to see my mother."

"Very well. You may go. You have worked hard," said his master,
and he gave Hans a lump of silver
as big as his head.

Hans went along the road.

"How lucky I am," he thought, but the lump of silver was heavy to carry.

Soon a man on a horse came along.

"That's a fine horse," said Hans. "I wish I had a horse instead of this lump of silver."

"I'll change with you," said the man. So he took the lump of silver and gave the horse to Hans. Hans was very glad. He rode the horse slowly. Then he went faster. Then he went so fast

that he fell off. Just then a boy
with a cow came that way.

"That's a fine cow," said Hans.
"I wish I had a cow
instead of this horse."

"I'll change with you," said the boy.
So he took the horse and gave the cow

to Hans. Hans was very glad.
He went along the road.
It was a hot day and he felt thirsty.

"I'll milk my cow," he thought.
He tried to milk her, but he couldn't
get a drop. Just then a man with a pig
came that way.

"That's a fine pig," said Hans.
"I wish I had a pig
instead of this cow."

"I'll change with you," said the man.
So he took the cow and gave the pig
to Hans. Hans was very glad. On he went
along the road. Soon a man with a white
goose came that way. When he saw
the pig he said,

"A pig was stolen from a sty not far
from here. If you are seen with that pig,
you'll be thrown into the duck pond."

"Oh, dear!" said Hans. "But I didn't
steal it. Please help me. Would you
change your white goose for my pig?"

So the man took the pig and gave the white goose to Hans. Hans was very glad. On he went along the road.

Soon he came to an old man who was rubbing a knife on a stone to make it sharp. As he worked, he sang.

"You are happy," said Hans.

"Yes," said the old man. "This is good work to do. I make a lot of money this way. But where did you get that white goose?"

"I gave a pig for it."

"Where did you get the pig?"

"I gave a cow for it."

"Where did you get the cow?"

"I gave a horse for it."

"Where did you get the horse?"

"I gave a lump of silver for it."

"Where did you get the silver?"

"I worked hard for seven years, and my master gave it to me."

"Ah!" said the old man. "Why don't

you change once more? Give me
your white goose for this stone.
Then you can sharpen knives.
It's good work. You can make a lot
of money that way."

So the old man took the white goose
and gave the stone to Hans. Hans was
very glad. On he went along the road,
but the stone was heavy to carry.

Soon he came to a pond.
He felt thirsty again.
He put the stone on the bank
and leaned over to drink.
He forgot the stone, and splash!
It fell into the pond.
Down, down it went to the bottom.

"Oh!" said Hans.
"Now I have nothing heavy to carry.
I am lucky!"

So on he went along the road,
till he came home to his mother.

Adapted

Pussy Willows

Have you seen Pussy Willows
in the springtime, growing on the twigs
like tiny balls of fur?
Have you ever said to yourself,
"I wonder how they came there?"
If you have, then this story is for you.
It is a very old story, about a rabbit.

Rabbit was going along by the stream
one day. Every time he came
to a small bush, or a branch hanging low,
he took a little run, and gave
a big jump over it.
One, two, three, jump!

First he jumped over a stone.
Then he jumped over a bush.
Then he jumped over a willow branch,
but there were some twigs sticking out
of the willow branch. As Rabbit jumped,
his tail caught on one of them.

He pulled. His tail stuck fast.
He tugged. His tail stuck fast.
He pulled and he tugged. He tugged and
he pulled, and off came his tail!
Down jumped Rabbit, but he didn't know
that he had left his tail behind
on the willow tree.

On he ran again, jumping as he went.
One, two, three, jump!
One, two, three, jump!

Soon he met Tortoise.

"Where's your tail?" asked Tortoise.

"Isn't it there?" said Rabbit.
He felt with his paw.
His white, fluffy tail had gone!

"Where can it be?" he said.

"You must have lost it," said Tortoise.
"I'll help you to look for it.
Which way did you come?"

"Along by the stream."

"Did you walk or run?"

"I ran—one, two, three, jump!"

"What did you jump over?"

"A stone."

"What else?"

"A bush."

"What else?"

"A willow branch. Ah! I must have lost it there."

Rabbit and Tortoise went back, along by the stream, till they came to the willow tree. There, caught on a twig, was Rabbit's tail. He took it down and put it on again.

"Now," said Tortoise when it had stuck, "you lost your tail on the willow tree, so the willow tree will have little white, fluffy tails in the springtime

from now on. Then people will always
know that you lost your tail on a willow
tree." Then he said goodbye,
and went on his way.

"Thank you," cried Rabbit, and he went
along by the stream, running and jumping.

One, two, three, jump!

One, two, three, jump!

That's the end of the story.
If it's true, then it's strange, isn't it,
that we don't call the little fluffy tails
Rabbit Willows, instead of Pussy Willows?

Adapted

Teddy the Koala

Say "ko-ah-la." It means "no drink." It is the name given to the fat, cuddly tree bears in Australia, because they never do drink.

Teddy was a koala. He lived in Australia a long time ago. In those days there were millions of koalas in Australia,

and there were lots and lots of forests
where they could live in peace.

When Teddy was a baby he was only
two centimetres long.
He spent all his time in his mother's
pouch.   There he was warm and safe.
He fed on his mother's milk,
and he slept most of the day
and most of the night.

His mother fed on the grey-green leaves
and the sweet young shoots
and the little stems and seed pods
of gum trees.

There are more than five hundred
different sorts of gum trees in Australia,
but only a few of them are good
for koalas.
Teddy's mother liked:
    manna gum
    yellow box gum
    swamp gum
and candlebark gum.

Teddy stayed in his mother's pouch
until he was nearly six months old.
Then he climbed out
and looked at the world around him.
He was a fine looking little koala
by that time.

His body was round and fat.
His grey-brown fur was thick and soft.
His claws were long and sharp.
His nose was like a bit
of black leather.
He looked like a toy teddy bear
come to life.

He did not often go back
into the pouch now,
but he clung to his mother's back
and rode everywhere with her.
In the daytime they usually slept
high in a tree, cuddled up together,
swaying a little among the leaves.
At night they usually walked
on the ground, looking for

the right sort of gum trees.

Teddy's mother gave him grey-green
leaves and sweet, young shoots to eat.
She gave him:
- manna gum
- yellow box gum
- swamp gum

and candlebark gum.

There were many other koalas
in the forest, but Teddy and his mother
hardly mixed with them at all.
For a long time they were very happy.

Then one day strange sounds filled
the air. Some men tramped about
and began to cut down the gum trees.
They were clearing the land for farms
and houses. They came day after day
with axes and noisy saws.

One tree after another
fell with a great crash.
All their leaves shivered and shook
and the forest was filled with sighing.

The koalas were afraid.
They scrambled to the ground
and hurried away.
Teddy clung to his mother's back.

There were other koalas all round
him. There were big old koalas
and small young ones
hurrying through the forest.
There were babies in their mothers'
pouches, and babies on their mothers'
backs. All the koalas were very afraid.

At last they came to another part
of the forest, far from the sound
of crashing trees.

"Now," said Teddy's mother
in her own way, "we can settle down
and live in peace once more."
But this was not so easy.
There were lots and lots of gum trees
but they were not the kind that are
good for koalas.

Teddy and his mother could not find any
- manna gum
- yellow box gum
- swamp gum

or candlebark gum.
They became thin and hungry.
The other koalas became thin and
hungry too. Many of them became ill
and many of them died.

Once there had been millions of koalas
but now there were only thousands.
People were taking more and more

of the forests for farms and houses.
They were cutting down more and more
trees, and sometimes their camp fires
set great stretches of bush alight.

Often and often Teddy and his mother
had to run on and on to look for
somewhere else to live.

Now about this time
the people of Australia began to think.
It was almost as if they had been asleep
and had just woken up.
They began to say to each other,

"This is the only country in the world
where koalas live.
They cannot even be sent to zoos
in other lands because it wouldn't
be possible to feed them properly.

We love our koalas but we are
not looking after them at all.
We used to have millions of them.
Now there are only a few thousand.
Soon there will be only a few hundred.

Then there will be only forty or fifty.
Then one day there will be none at all.

We cut down their gum trees
so that we can make farms and build
houses and towns. We start camp fires
that spread and become great bush fires.
Some people even kill the koalas and
sell their fur coats. We must
do something to save our koalas."

Some of the people met together
and made a plan. They planned to catch
a few hundred koalas and take them
to an island just off the south coast.
It was called Phillip Island.
Lots of gum trees grew there. There was:
>   manna gum
>
>   yellow box gum
>
>   swamp gum

and candlebark gum.

There were also beautiful wild birds
and Fairy Penguins, the smallest penguins
in the world.

There were seals too,
hundreds and hundreds of them
lying on the rocks out at sea.
Phillip Island was quiet and peaceful.
The koalas would be safe there.

So once more some men went into
the forests where the koalas
were living.
Teddy and his mother were high in a tree.
They were cuddled up together
half asleep, swaying a little
among the leaves. They were very thin

and weak and ill. They did not even see
a man below holding a long pole
with a net on the end.

Suddenly the net was slipped over
the koalas' heads.
Teddy's mother tried to struggle free
and she began to climb down the tree
to escape. Teddy clung to her
and struck out with his claws,
but the net was tangled round the koalas
and they could not escape.

A few moments later they were pushed
into a wooden box with slits at the sides
so that they could see out.
They were filled with fear and terror.
They didn't know that people were
helping them. The box was lifted
on to a lorry, and other boxes
with other koalas were stacked up
beside them.

Then the lorry began its journey,
and the koalas were very afraid.

After a while Teddy and his mother
fell asleep, so they didn't know
that the lorry went over a long bridge
to an island. In any case
they would not have understood at all
what was happening to them.

Then suddenly they both awoke.
They saw that the box was open again
at one end, and a big patch of bright
sunlight was shining in on them.

"Come on," said someone kindly.
"Out you go."
Teddy jumped on to his mother's back,
and she stumbled out into the fresh air.
A man gave her a gentle push
and she smelled the smell of gum trees.

"Gum trees!" squeaked Teddy in his
own way.
He clung to his mother's thick, soft fur
and she hurried forward to the forest
in front of them.

It was daytime, and koalas

usually sleep in the daytime,
but Teddy and his mother were hungry,
and here they saw gum trees. There was:
> manna gum
>
> yellow box gum
>
> swamp gum

and candlebark gum.

Swiftly Teddy's mother scrambled up
a manna gum tree. She pulled pawfuls
of leaves and sweet young shoots,
and stuffed them into Teddy's mouth
and into her own.

This was Phillip Island where there were
beautiful wild birds and Fairy Penguins,
the smallest penguins in the world.
There were seals too,
hundreds and hundreds of them
lying on the rocks out at sea.

This was Phillip Island, where Teddy
and his mother were to live safely
and happily for the rest of their lives.

All the koalas settled so happily

there that they soon grew well
and strong again.

There are still hundreds
of them on Phillip Island, but there are
now thousands of koalas in other
parts of Australia too. This is because
laws have been made to protect them.

Now Australian people take great care
of their koalas.
They know that Australia
is the only country in the world
where koalas can live.

Sun and Wind

It was one of those days
when no one was quite sure
what the weather was going to be.

One moment it was hot.
The next moment it was cold.
One moment the sun was shining.
The next moment the wind was blowing.

Up in the sky, the sun
and the wind were talking.

This is what they were saying.

Wind: I shall blow,
and make everyone cold.

Sun : I shall shine,
and warm them up again.

Wind: If I blow, you can't shine.
I shall blow clouds over you,
and hide you.

Sun : I shall send my sunbeams
peeping through your clouds.

Wind: But I am stronger than you.

Everyone knows that the wind
is stronger than the sun.
Sun : No, no. I am stronger than you.
Everyone knows that the sun
is stronger than the wind.
Wind: We'll have a test.
Look on the street down there.
Can you see a man
with a brown coat?
Sun : Yes.
Wind: We'll see who can take off
his coat.
Sun : All right. You go first.
Wind: I'll blow it off.
Whoo whoo whoo!
Sun : You're making him cold.
He's doing up his buttons.
Wind: Whoo whoo whoo!
Sun : He's turning up his collar.
You can't take off his coat.
Now it's my turn.
Wind: You won't be able to do it

by shining.

Sun : See how warm I'm making him.
He's turning down his collar.

Wind: He's undoing his buttons.

Sun : He's taking off his coat!

Wind: It's off! You have won!

The wind was so surprised at this
that he hurried off,
and blew away the clouds.
This left the sun alone in the sky
to shine as brightly as he wished.

Then everyone looked up and said,
"What a lovely day!"

Adapted